THE HOSTILE SUN · *the poetry of d. h. lawrence*

THE HOSTILE SUN · *the poetry of d. h. lawrence*

Black Sparrow Press
los angeles · 1973

Acknowledgement is made to *American Review* and
Massachusetts Review where parts of this essay were first published.

LIBRARY OF CONGRESS CATALOGING IN PUBLICATION DATA

Oates, Joyce Carol, 1938-
    The hostile sun.

    Includes bibliographical references.
    1. Lawrence, David Herbert, 1885-1930. I. Title.
PR6023.A93Z757   821'.9'12   73-8763
ISBN 0-87685-169-3 (signed cloth ed.)
ISBN 0-87685-168-5 (pbk.)

                    Black Sparrow Press
                    P.O. Box 25603
                    Los Angeles, California
                    90025

THE HOSTILE SUN

The Poetry of D. H. Lawrence

I am that I am
from the sun
and people are not my measure.

—*"Aristocracy of the Sun"*

Lawrence's poems are blunt, exasperating, impos-
ing upon us his strangely hectic, strangely delicate
music, in fragments, in tantalizing broken-off parts
of a whole too vast to be envisioned—and then with-
drawing again. They are meant to be spontaneous
works, spontaneously experienced; they are not meant
to give us the sense of grandeur or permanence which
other poems attempt, the fallacious sense of immor-
tality that is an extension of the poet's ego. Yet they
achieve a kind of immortality precisely in this: that
they transcend the temporal, the intellectual. They are
ways of experiencing the ineffable "still point" which
Eliot could approach only through abstract language.

It is illuminating to read Lawrence's entire poetic
work as a kind of journal, in which not only the

7

finished poems themselves but variants and early drafts and uncollected poems constitute a strange unity—an autobiographical novel, perhaps—that begins with "The quick sparks" and ends with "immortal bird." This massive work is more powerful, more emotionally combative, than even the greatest of his novels. Between first and last line there is literally everything: beauty, waste, "flocculent ash," the ego in a state of rapture and in a state of nausea, a diverse streaming of chaos and cunning. We know that Yeats fashioned his "soul" in the many-volumed *Collected Works of W. B. Yeats* quite consciously, systematically, and Lawrence has unconsciously and unsystematically created a similar work. It is shameless, in part; but there are moments of beauty in it that are as powerful as Yeats's more frequent moments. There are moments of clumsiness, ugliness, and sheer stubborn spite, quite unredeemed by any poetic grace, so much so, in fact, that the number of excellent poems is therefore all the more amazing. Ultimately, Lawrence forces us to stop judging each individual poem. The experience of reading all the poems—and their earlier forms—becomes a kind of mystical appropriation of Lawrence's life, *or life itself,* in which the essential sacredness of "high" and "low," "beauty" and "ugliness," "poetry" and "nonpoetry" is celebrated in a magical transcendence of all rationalist dichotomies.

8

I. THE CANDID REVELATION: Lawrence's Aesthetics

Lawrence is one of our true prophets, not only in his "madness for the unknown" and in his explicit warning—

> If we do not rapidly open all the doors of con-
> sciousness
> and freshen the putrid little space in which we
> are cribbed
> the sky-blue walls of our unventilated heaven
> will be bright red with blood.
>> ("Nemesis," from *Pansies*)

—but in his life-long development of a technique, a fictional and poetic *way* in which the prophetic voice can be given formal expression. It is a technique that refuses to study itself closely, that refuses to hint at its position in any vast cultural tradition— how unlike that of Eliot, for instance!—and that refuses, even, most unforgivably to the serious-minded, to take itself seriously. Richard Aldington, writing in 1932, contrasts Lawrence's delight in the imperfect with James Joyce's insistence upon perfection, and though Aldington seems overly biased against Joyce, his point about Lawrence is well made. Lawrence was not interested in that academic, adolescent, and rather insane human concept of "The Perfect," knowing very well that dichotomies like Perfect/Imperfect are only invented by men according to their cultural or political or emotional dispositions, and then imposed upon others. Everything changes, says Lawrence; most of all, standards of apparently immutable taste, aesthetic standards of perfection that are soon left behind by the spontaneous flow of life.

Therefore he strikes us as very contemporary—moody and unpredictable and unreliable—a brilliant performer when he cares to be, but quite maliciously willing to inform us of the dead spaces, the blanks in his imagination. Not a finer poet than Yeats, Lawrence is often much more sympathetic; he seems to be demonstrating in his very style, in the process of writing his poetry, the revelation that comes at the conclusion of Yeats's "The Circus Animals' Desertion" (a poem that itself comes near the conclusion of Yeats's great body of work)—the knowledge that the poet, for all his higher wisdom, must lie down "where all the ladders start,/ In the

10

foul rag-and-bone shop of the heart." Yet it has always seemed to me ironic that this revelation comes to us in a poem that is technically perfect—a Platonic essence of what a poem should be. By contrast, Lawrence seems to be writing, always writing, out of the abrupt, ungovernable impulses of his soul, which he refuses to shape into an art as perfected as Yeats's. He would have scorned the idea of hoping for either a perfection of life or of art—he is more like one of us.

But critics, especially "New Critics" and "Formalist Critics," have not understood this: that there are many kinds of art, that there may be a dozen, a hundred ways of writing, and that no single way is the ultimate way. Lawrence was exasperated by, but not deeply influenced by, the stupidity of his critics; but it may be harder for us, in reading an essay like R. P. Blackmur's "Lawrence and Expressive Form" (in *Language as Gesture,* 1954) to restrain our impatience. Blackmur states that Lawrence is guilty of writing "fragmentary biography" instead of "poetry." It would have been unthinkable to imagine that the two are not separate . . . ? need not be separate . . . ? And what does "poetry," that elusive, somehow punitive term, mean to Blackmur? If we read farther we see that his definition of "poetry" is simply his expectation of what poetry *must* be, based on the poets he has evidently read, and judged wor-

11

thy of the title of "poet." One needs the "structures of art," which are put there by something Blackmur calls a "rational imagination." All this suggests that the critic is in control of what is rational, and if one investigates far enough he learns that this critic is unhappy because Lawrence the "craftsman" did not often enough silence Lawrence the demon of "personal outburst." Lawrence leaves us, therefore, only with "the ruins of great intentions." I mention this because it is symptomatic of academic criticism at its most sinister, since its assumptions are so hidden that one can hardly discover them. But when they are brought to light it becomes clear that the critic is punishing the poet for not being a form of the critic himself, a kind of analogue to his ego. It is a method of suppression that passes for rational discourse, "objective" criticism; a colleague of mine once stated that *Moby Dick* is a "failure" because it does not "live up to" the form of the "novel."

For Lawrence, of course, art antedates any traditional form. He is fascinated by the protean nature of reality, the various possibilities of the ego. Throughout the entire collection of poems there is a deep, unshakable faith in the transformable quality of all life. Even the elegaic "The Ship of Death" (written as Lawrence was dying) ends with a renewal, in typically Laurentian words: ". . . and the whole thing starts again." Like most extraordinary

12

men, Lawrence is concerned with directing the way his writing will be assessed; the ambitious are never content to leave the writing of their biographies to others, who may make mistakes. So he says, in a prefatory note in 1928, "No poetry, not even the best, should be judged as if it existed in the absolute, in the vacuum of the absolute. Even the best poetry, when it is at all personal, needs the penumbra of its own time and place and circumstance to make it full and whole." Surely this is correct, and yet it is a point missed by most critics, and not just critics of Lawrence, who assume that their subjects are "subjects" and not human beings, and that their works of art are somehow crimes, for which they are on perpetual trial.

The critic who expects to take up Lawrence's poems and read poems by T. S. Eliot, for instance, is wasting everyone's time. Lawrence's poems are for people who want to experience the poetic process as well as its product, who want the worst as well as the best, because they are infinitely curious about the man, the human being, D. H. Lawrence himself. If you love someone it is a total engagement; if you wish to be transformed into him, as one is into Lawrence, you must expect rough treatment. That is one of the reasons why Lawrence has maddened so many people—they sense his violent, self-defining magic, which totally excludes them and makes them irrelevant, unless they "become" Lawrence himself, on his terms and not their own.

He trusted himself, endured and suffered himself, worked his way through himself (sometimes only barely) and came through—"look! we have come through!"—and he expects no less of his readers. Only a spiritual brother or sister of Lawrence himself can understand his poems, ultimately; this is why we strain upward, puzzled by yearning for an equality with him, if only in flashes. We need a violent distending of our imaginations in order to understand him. It is almost a reversal of Nietzsche's remark, to the effect that one must have the "permission" of one's envious friends, in order to be acknowledged as great: Lawrence might have felt that one's friends must earn the permission of recognizing that he, Lawrence, *is* a great man.

There is a deadly little poem called "Blank" in which Lawrence says coldly: "At present I am a blank, and I admit it./ . . . So I am just going to go on being a blank, till something nudges me from within,/ and makes me know I am not blank any longer." The poems themselves are nudges, some sharp and cruel and memorable indeed, most of them a structured streaming of consciousness, fragments of a total self that could not always keep up the strain of totality. Sometimes Lawrence was anguished over this, but most of the time he believed that in his poetry, as in life itself, what must be valued is the springing-forth of the natural, forcing its own organic shape, not forced into a preordained structure. He is much more fluid and inventive than the Imagists, whose work resembles some of his cooler, shorter poems, in his absolute commitment to the honoring of his own creative processes. Picasso has stated that it is his own dynamism he is painting, because the movement of his thought interests him more than the thought itself, and while Lawrence does not go this far, something of the same is true in his utilisation and valuing of spontaneity. He says:

> Ours is the universe of the unfolded rose,
> The explicit,
> The candid revelation.

So Lawrence declares and defines himself, and the impersonal in himself (which he valued, of course, more than the "personal"), in a word-for-word, line-by-line, poem-by-poem sequence of revelations.

For Lawrence, as for Nietzsche, it is the beauty and mystery of flux, of "Becoming," that enchants us; not permanence, not "Being." Permanence exists only in the conscious mind. It is a structure erected to perfection, therefore airless and stultifying. Lawrence says in a letter of 1913, written to Ernest Collings, from Italy:

I conceive a man's body as a kind of flame, like a candle flame, forever upright and yet flowing: and the intellect is just the light that is shed on to the things around. And I am not so much concerned with the things around—which is really mind—but with the mystery of the flame forever flowing. . . . We have got so ridiculously mindful, that we never know that we ourselves are anything—we think there are only the objects we shine upon. And there the poor flame goes on burning ignored, to produce this light. And instead of chasing the mystery in the fugitive, half-lighted things outside us, we ought to look at ourselves, and say, "My God, I am myself!"

(*Collected Letters*, I, 180.)

This is exactly contemporary with us: except now, at last, men whose training has been scientific and positivistic and clinical and "rational" (the most obvious being R. D. Laing, Abraham Maslow, Buckminster Fuller) are beginning to say the same thing. And, like Maslow—but unlike Freud—Lawrence would assert that the so-called "destructive instincts" are really a manifestation of intellectual perversion, not healthy instinct. Lawrence's arrogant prophetic stance in "The Revolutionary" ("see if I don't bring you down, and all your high opinion/. . . Your particular

16

heavens,/ With a smash.") is becoming justified.

Lawrence loves the true marriage of heaven and hell, illusory opposites, he loves to exalt the apparently unbeautiful. For instance, in the poem "Medlars and Sorb-Apples" (from his best single volume of poems, *Birds, Beasts, and Flowers,* of 1923), he says:

> I love you, rotten,
> Delicious rottenness.
>
> I love to suck you out from your skins
> So brown and soft and coming suave,
> So morbid. . . .

He sees these fruits as "autumnal excrementa" and they please him very much. Earlier in a poem called "Craving for Spring," he has declared that he is sick of the flowers of earliest spring—the snowdrops, the jonquils, the "chill Lent lilies" because of their "faint-bloodedness,/ slow-blooded, icy-fleshed" purity. He would like to trample them underfoot. (What is remarkable in Lawrence's "nature" poems is his fierce, combative, occasionally peevish relationship with birds, beasts, and flowers—he does them the honor, as the Romantic poets rarely did, of taking them seriously.) So much for the virgins, so much for portentousness! It is with a totally different emotion that he approaches the sorb-apples, a kind of worship, a dread:

17

Gods nude as blanched nut-kernels,
Strangely, half-sinisterly flesh-fragrant
As if with sweat,
and drenched with mystery.

. . . .

I say, wonderful are the hellish experiences,
Orphic, delicate
Dionysos of the Underworld.

A kiss, and a spasm of farewell, a moment's
    orgasm of rupture,
Then along the damp road alone, till the next
    turning.
And there, a new partner, a new parting, a new
    unfusing into twain,
A new gasp of further isolation . . . .

These poems are remarkable in that they refuse to
state, with the kind of godly arrogance we take for
granted in Shakespeare, that they will confer any
immortality on their subjects. As Lawrence says in
his short essay, "Poetry of the Present" (1918), he
is not attempting the "treasured, gem-like lyrics of
Shelley and Keats," though he values them. His
poetry is like Whitman's, a poetry of the "pulsating,
carnal self," and therefore Lawrence celebrates the
falling-away, the rotting, the transient, even the
slightly sinister, and above all his own proud isola-
tion, "Going down the strange lanes of hell, more

and more intensely alone," until hell itself is some-
how made exquisite:

> Each soul departing with its own isolation,
> Strangest of all strange companions,
> And best.

In 1929, Lawrence says in his foreword to
Pansies: "A flower passes, and that perhaps is the
best of it. If we can take it in its transience, its breath,
its maybe mephistophelian, maybe palely ophelian
face, the look it gives, the gesture of its full bloom,
and the way it turns upon us to depart," we will have
been faithful to it, and not simply to our own pro-
jected egos. Immortality, he says, can give us nothing
to compare with this. The poems that make up
Pansies are "merely the breath of the moment, and
one eternal moment easily contradicting the next
eternal moment." The extraordinary word is *eternal*.
Lawrence reveals himself as a mystic by this casual,
off-hand critical commentary on his own work, as
much as he does in the work itself. He can experience
the eternal *in* the temporal, and he realizes, as few
people do, that the temporal is eternal by its very
nature: as if a piece of colored glass were held up to
the sun, becoming sacred as it is illuminated by the
sun, but also making the sun itself sacred. To Law-
rence, the sun is a symbol of the ferocious externality

19

of nature, the uncontrollable, savage Otherness of nature, which must be recognized, honored, but not subdued—as if man could subdue it, except by deceiving himself. The sun is "hostile," yet a mystic recognizes the peculiar dependency of the eternal upon the temporal; the eternal being is made "real" or realized only through the temporal. Someday it may be taken for granted that the "mystical vision" and "common sense" are not opposed, that one is simply an extension of the other, but, because it represents a natural development not actually realized by most people, it is said to be opposed to logical thought.

There is a rhythmic, vital relationship between the Eternal and the Temporal, the one pressing close upon the other, not remote and cold, but mysteriously close. Lawrence says in "Mutilation,"

> I think I could alter the frame of things in my agony.
> I think I could break the System with my heart.
> I think, in my convulsion, the skies would break.

Inner and outer reality are confused, rush together, making up a pattern of harmony and discord, which is Lawrence's basic vision of the universe and the controlling aesthetics behind his poetry. It is significant that when Lawrence seems to us at his very worst—

20

in *The Plumed Serpent, Kangaroo,* much of *Apocalypse,* nearly all of the poems in *Nettles* and *More Pansies*—he is stridently dogmatic, authoritative, speaking without ambiguity or mystery, stating and not suggesting, as if attempting to usurp the position of the Infinite (and unknowable), putting everything into packaged forms. When he seems to us most himself, he is more fragmentary, more spontaneous, inspired to write because of something he has encountered in the outside world—a "nudge" to his blankness, a stimulus he is startled by, as he is by the hummingbird in the poem of that title, imagining it as a jabbing, prehistorical monster, now seen through the wrong end of the telescope; or as he is by a doe in "A Doe at Evening," when he thinks:

> Ah yes, being male, is not my head hard-
> balanced, antlered?
> Are not my haunches light?
> Has she not fled on the same wind with me?
> Does not my fear cover her fear?

Questions, and not answers, are Lawrence's real technique, just as the process of thinking is his subject matter, not any formalized structures of "art." Because of this he is one of the most vital of all poets, in his presentation of himself as the man who wonders, who asks questions, who feels emotions of joy or misery or fury, the man who *reacts,* coming up hard against things in a real world, both the creator of poems and the involuntary creation of the stimuli he has encountered—that is, he is so nudged by life that he must react, he must be altered, scorning the protection of any walls of "reason" or "tradition" that might make experience any less painful.

Typically, he is fascinated by "unissued, uncanny America," in the poem "The Evening Land," confessing that he is half in love, half horrified, by the "demon people/lurking among the deeps of your industrial thicket"—in fact, he is allured by these demons, who have somehow survived the America of machines:

> Say, in the sound of all your machines
> And white words, white-wash American,
> Deep pulsing of a strange heart
> New throb, like a stirring under the false dawn
> that precedes the real.
> Nascent American
> Demonish, lurking among the undergrowth
> Of many-stemmed machines and chimneys that
> smoke like pine-trees.

For Lawrence, America itself is a question.

II. NEW HEAVEN AND EARTH: Lawrence's Transformations

In Lawrence we experience the paradox—made dramatic by his genius—of a brilliant man trying to resist his own brilliance, his own faculty for dividing, categorizing, assessing, making clear and conscious and therefore finite. It seems almost a dark angel of his, this dreaded "consciousness," and he wrestles with it throughout his life, stating again and again that we are "godless" when we are "full of thought," that consciousness leads to mechanical evil, to self-consciousness, to nullity. He yearned for the separateness of an individual isolation, somehow in conjunction with another human being—a woman—but not dependent upon this person, mysteriously absolved of any corrupting "personal" bond. It is the "pulsating, carnal self" he wants to isolate, not the rational self, the activity of the personality-bound ego he came to call, in a late poem called "Only

23

Man," the "self-apart-from-god"— his only projection of a real hell, a fathomless fall into the abyss:

> For the knowledge of the self-apart-from-God
> is an abyss down which the soul can slip
> writhing and twisting in all the revolutions
> of the unfinished plunge
> of self-awareness, now apart from God, falling
> fathomless, fathomless, self-consciousness
>   wriggling
> writhing deeper and deeper in all the minutiae
>   of self-knowledge, downwards, exhaustive,
> yet never, never coming to the bottom . . . .

He uses his intellect not to demolish the mind's attempts at order, as David Hume did, but to insist upon the limits of any activity of "pure" reason—to retain the sacred, unknowable part of the self that Kant called the Transcendental Ego, the Ego above the personal, which is purely mental and sterile. So intent is he upon subjecting the "personal" to the "impersonal" that he speaks impatiently of tragedy, which is predicated upon an assumption of the extraordinary worth of certain individuals, and there is in his mind a curious and probably unique equation between the exalted pretensions of tragedy and the rationalizing, de-sacralizing process he sensed in operation everywhere around him, in scientific method, in education, in industry, in the financial network of nations, even in new methods of war which resulted not in killing but in commonplace murder. Where to many people tragedy as an art form or an attitude toward life might be dying because belief in God is dying, to Lawrence tragedy is impure, representative of a distorted claim to prominence in the universe, a usurpation of the sacredness of the Other, the Infinite. Throughout his life he exhibits a fascination with the drama of the self and its totally Other, not an Anti-Self, to use Yeats's vocabulary, but a truly foreign life-force, symbolized by the sun in its healthy hostility to man. It is a remarkable battle, fought for decades, Lawrence the abrasive, vitally-alive individual for some reason absorbed in a struggle to deny the primacy of the individual, the "catastrophe" of personal feeling.[1] Why this battle, why this obsession? Why must he state in so many different ways the relatively simple thought here expressed in "Climb Down, O Lordly Mind"?—

> The blood knows in darkness, and forever dark,
> in touch, by intuition, instinctively.
> The blood also knows religiously,
> and of this the mind is incapable.
> The mind is non-religious.
>
> To my dark heart, gods *are*.

In my dark heart, love is and is not.
But to my white mind
gods and love alike are but an idea,
a kind of fiction.

Calvin Bedient in a brilliant study of Lawrence
argues that his flight from personality had been, in
part, an effort to "keep himself separate from others
so as to be free to face the 'beyond' where his moth-
er had become 'intermingled.' "[2] Because of this, his
mysticism is "somewhat morbid." But the mystic in
Lawrence is fierce to insist upon salvation, even in
the face of madness and dissolution, when the mere-
ly mental might give way. It is significant that the
delirious fever Ursula suffers at the very end of *The
Rainbow* brings her to a mystic certainty of her
strength, her unbreakable self; if it is deathly—she
evidently suffers a miscarriage—it is not *her* death,
not Lawrence's idea of death at all. Ursula's real or
hallucinatory terror of the horses (that attempt to run
her down in a field) is the means by which she is
"saved," absolved of Skrebensky's child, which is to
her and to Lawrence hardly more than a symbol of the
finite, the deathly personal and limited. Nothing in
Lawrence is without ambiguity, but it is possible that
much that seems to us morbid is really Lawrence's
brutal insistence upon the separation of one part of
the self from the other, the conscious self from the

26

unconscious, and both from the truly external, the unknown and unknowable Infinite.

In the cycle of confessional poems called *Look! We Have Come Through!* (1917) the most important poem is the mysterious, yet explicit "New Heaven and Earth," which invites reading in a simplistic manner, as another of the love poems—indeed, Lawrence does more harm than good with his prefatory foreword and "argument" when he suggests that the sequence of poems is about a young man who "marries and comes into himself." Certainly the spiritual crisis Lawrence suffered at this time had something to do with his private life, with the circumstances of his elopement, but not all marriage is attended by such a radical convulsion of the soul. Lawrence's marriage, like everything else in his life, must be considered epiphenomenal in relationship to the deeper, less personal emotions he attempts to comprehend. This poem bears a curious resemblance to the beautiful late poem, "Ship of Death," though it is about a mystical re-affirmation of life.

"New Heaven and Earth" consists of eight stanzas, the first stating that the poet has crossed into "another world" where unknown people will misunderstand his weeping. It is not clear until the very end of the poem that the "unknown world" is really the ordinary world, which he re-experiences as totally new. He has passed over into an interior dimension of the sacred, he has evidently experienced the kind of absolute spiritual conversion we find recorded so often in history—the undesired, perhaps dreaded re-arrangement of all prior thought. But he must still talk about his experience in ordinary language, which the people around him will not understand "because it is quite, quite foreign to them." This is the problem for Lawrence, as it is for any mystic: he must use ordinary language, but he must use it to express an extraordinary event (unless he chooses, as Thomas Merton declares the poet must, to separate entirely his mystical life from his life as an artist). This might account for much of Lawrence's notorious impatience and contempt for most of humanity, certainly for organized religion and morality, since there is nothing more frustrating than hearing people speak casually and glibly of experiences they have not had personally, and of whose meaning they are therefore unaware. Anyone—and today nearly everyone—can speak of the "expansion of one's consciousness," the "transcendental experience," the "mystic vision," until these terms become meaningless, mere commodities. Yet anyone who has had such a vision is seared by it, his personality totally changed, and it would be impossible for him to revert back to an earlier, more "personal" self, even if he wanted to; one thinks of the certainty, the almost egoless egoism of Rousseau, who said that a topic for an essay competition catapulted him into another personality: "From the moment I read these words . . . I beheld another world and became another man."

For Lawrence, the shattering experience of a totally new vision had no clear, single cause that he has recorded. It is rather a downward, deathly movement to despair, a psychopathological experience that seems in his case to have been characterized by an exaggerated sense of his own "self," the hard unkillable selfish kernel of Being so coolly and affirmatively described in the short story, "The Princess."[3] This sinking into despair sometimes takes the form of the ego's terror of dissolution—not simply physical death, but immediate psychic dissolution, difficult to describe if one has not felt it, and Lawrence elsewhere (notably in the chapter called "Sunday Evening" in *Women in Love,* but only at the beginning of the chapter—the very Laurentian Ursula reasons her way out of it) explores this terror also. But the locked-in horror of the unkillable self seems to have been closer to Lawrence's own experience:

I was so weary of the world,
I was so sick of it,
everything was tainted with myself. . . .

I shall never forget the maniacal horror of it all
    in the end

29

when everything was me, I knew it all already, I
        anticipated it all in my soul
because I was the author and the result
I was the God and the creation at once;
creator, I looked at my creation;
created, I looked at myself, the creator:
it was a maniacal horror in the end.

It is instructive, Lawrence's quite casual use of the
expression "in the end"; clearly, whatever happened
to him was a kind of death, and he came to the end
of one phase of his life. If he had endured in his self-
ness, like Gerald Crich of *Women in Love,* he would
have lived out the rest of his life in his mind, this
mind being, horribly, "a bubble floating in the dark-
ness." But of course Gerald has not much of a life
remaining to him; the world becomes so loathsome
that he commits a kind of suicide, not just in rushing
out into the cold but in falling in love with his exact
counterpart, the life-fearing Gudrun. Gerald seems to
recognize his psychic predicament, but cannot cross
over into another world—he is "mechanical" man,
doomed to die in a vacuum. The recognition of the
"maniacal horror" is not enough to force a conver-
sion, as, sadly, it rarely is:

Life, friends, is boring. We must not say so.
After all, the sky flashes, the great sea yearns,

we ourselves flash and yearn,
and moreover my mother told me as a boy
(repeatingly) "Ever to confess you're bored
means you have no

Inner Resources." I conclude now I have no
inner resources, because I am heavy bored.

The voice is, of course, John Berryman's, the voice
he had to endure inside his head, stating and re-
stating the dimensions of that head, the recounting
of experiences become memories, only inside the
head, the immutable imprisoning skull. And here
is another voice, ultimately more savage than Berry-
man's:

. . . Is there no way out of the mind?
Steps at my back spiral into a well.
There are no trees or birds in this world,
There is only a sourness.

This is Sylvia Plath (in "Apprehensions"), and else-
where, in her autobiographical novel *The Bell Jar,*
she speaks candidly of the horror of this sourness,
the same stale sour air breathed in and out, though
she is a young woman with obvious gifts, an obvious
"life" to live—yet doomed.

But Lawrence felt a basic revulsion for suicide,

which is expressed in a poem in *Pansies* called "What Matters," where at the conclusion of a catalogue of sleazy thrills he has his speaker say:

> After that, of course, there's suicide—certain
> aspects, perhaps,
> Yes, I should say the contemplation of clever
> suicide *is* rather thrilling,
> so long as the thing is done neatly, and the world
> is left looking very fooled.

But this is another of Lawrence's voices, itself cerebral and glib. In "New Heaven and Earth" the tone is awed, reverential, the language continually straining its boundaries, in an effort to make the strangeness of his experience coherent. But he can only use generalized words, phrases, pseudo-dramatic actions:

> I buried my beloved; it was good, I buried
> myself and was gone.
> War came, and every hand raised to murder;
> very good, very good, every hand raised to
> murder!

He shares in the apocalyptic madness of the war, imagining himself as part of the era's murderousness, and then finds himself trodden out, gone, dead, reduced "absolutely to nothing." But, somehow, he then experiences a resurrection, "risen, not born again, but risen, body the same as before/. . . here, in the other world, still terrestrial/myself, the same as before, yet unaccountably new."

The deathly ennui is sloughed off, magically, and Lawrence finds that he is "mad for the unknown." A miracle has taken place, but it cannot be explained, only experienced:

> I, in the sour black tomb, trodden to absolute
> death
> I put out my hand in the night, one night, and
> my hand
> touched that which was verily not me. . . .

Perhaps the depth and passion of Lawrence's self-disgust were enough to get him through, or his religious notion that it is "the" death and not "his" death he awaits . . . ? In any case, a transformation occurs:

> Ha, I was a blaze leaping up!
> I was a tiger bursting into sunlight.
> I was greedy, I was mad for the unknown.
> I, new-risen, resurrected, starved from the tomb,
> starved from a life of devouring always
> myself. . . .

It is important to see that, in the seventh stanza, the poet touches his wife *after* his conversion; the wife herself, with whom he has lain "for over a thousand nights," is clearly outside the experience and outside the poem. He touches her after he is "carried by the current in death/ over to the new world," but, newly-transformed, he will not be able to explain what has happened. He will be a "madman in rapture" and the poem ends with a celebration of mystery, the "unknown, strong current of life supreme," the core of "utter mystery."

Why Lawrence is one of the survivors and not one of the many who, confronted with this kind of despair, force their own deaths in one way or another, is a question probably unanswerable, since it brings us to a consideration of the ultimate mystery of human personality. Perhaps it is Lawrence's reverence for all life, even his own sickly and self-consuming life, that allows this experience—whatever it is—to take possession of him; he does not attempt a false possession of it. Lawrence, to be true to himself, to his deepest self, must allow the "drowning," the near-annihilation, the sweeping of the soul back to the primitive "sources of mystery."

An earlier poem, "Humiliation," more clearly related to Lawrence's private life, suggests this same attitude—a reluctant but permanent acceptance of the power of something apart from him. It is painful, horrible, humiliating, but it is probably what saves Lawrence from utter despair, off and on during his troubled life:

> God, that I have no choice!
> That my own fulfilment is up against me
> Timelessly!
> The burden of self-accomplishment!
> The charge of fulfilment!
> And God, that she is *necessary!*
> *Necessary,* and I have no choice!

(It is interesting to compare the idyllic lyricism of such poems as "Wedlock" and "Song of a Man Who is Loved" with the rhetorical frenzy of a poem like "Humiliation"—assuming, with Lawrence, that both attitudes toward his beloved are normal, and must be expressed.) One is struck again and again by Lawrence's moral courage, his stubborn faith in the processes of life, the sweeping currents of life, which force him on to new visions *even against his instinctive will,* at times; he never loses the initial vision that makes incidental suffering bearable—

> There are said to be creative pauses,
> pauses that are as good as death, empty and dead
>   as death itself.
> And in these awful pauses the evolutionary

change takes place.

("Nullus")

Such poems as "The Death of our Era," "The New World," "Nemesis," "A Played-Out Game," and many others, remind us of Yeats's dramatic use of the individual poet enduring his age's spiritual exhaustion, but transcending it, through a mystical affinity for the age to come, achieved only through some apocalyptic upheaval of civilization. In "The Hostile Sun," included in the generally disappointing volume *More Pansies,* Lawrence speaks of the terror of the sun, its opposition to man's finite consciousness, whose "thoughts are stiff, like old leaves/ and ideas . . . hard, like acorns ready to fall." The sun, which is the source of all life, is too powerful, too savage, for ordinary diminished men. Proper dread of it is a way of honoring the unknowable in the universe, and the unknowable deep in the self:

> . . . we suffer, and though the sun bronzes us
> we feel him strangling even more the issues of
>   our soul
> for he is hostile to all the leafy foliage of our
>   thoughts
> and the old upward flowing of our sap, the pres-
>   sure of our upward flow of feeling
> is against him.

Understanding this hostility, man must retreat to the calmness of the moon, to its strange sinister "calm of scimitars and brilliant reaping hooks"; there, peace is possible. But peace for Lawrence usually signals a kind of death, and the only noble human gesture is a brave affirmation of the sun's inhuman powers:

> I am that I am
> from the sun,
> and people are not my measure.
> ("Aristocracy of the Sun")

In Lawrence's finest sustained sequence of poems, *Birds, Beasts, and Flowers,* he honors the unknowable mysteries of other forms of life, some of them as disturbing in their ways as the sun itself. Lawrence is really unlike any poet one can call to mind, in his utter absorption with the "other," which goes far beyond the kind of Negative Capability Keats demonstrated in his poetry. He is not trying to project himself into these creatures, nor is he trying, really, to interpret them. They remain alien, brute, essentially unknowable. They exist in their own absolute realms of being, separate from him, though they may become temporarily symbolic during the course of a poem, as in "Snake," where the snake's observed godliness is transformed into "that part of him that was left behind [convulsing] in undignified haste"—

37

Lawrence's destruction of the god in the snake, hence the "god" in himself, for which he is ashamed.

"Humming-bird" is an exotic, highly imaginative poem in which the poet envisions the bird in a primeval-dumb world, in an "awful stillness" before "anything had a soul, / While life was a heave of Matter. . . ." The humming-bird, apparently so fragile, is seen as flashing ahead of creation, piercing "the slow vegetable veins with his long beak." Man, seeing him today, is really observing him through the wrong end of the long telescope of Time—in his original state he was enormous, a huge jabbing monster. This bizarre vision might have been experienced by any Symbolist or Expressionist poet, but only Lawrence could have rejoiced at the nightmare image he has created. And only Lawrence, in contemplating the energies of "The He-Goat," could have shrewdly observed the diminished egoism of that "black procreant male of the selfish will," enslaved to the female, and therefore to the herd. The mindless submission to one's own selfish will, though it appears to be an acquiescence to natural instinct, becomes only a mechanical frenzy, a domestication, when the true object of desire—the "enemy," the "Other"—has been removed. Thus the male goat has no natural enemy, being king of his herd of indifferent females; all the other males have been removed from his world, and he is left in the "sullen-stagnating atmosphere of goats"—

> . . . Like a big ship pushing her bowsprit over
>   the little ships
> Then swerving and steering afresh
> And never, never arriving at journey's end, at
>   the rear of the female ships.

In a natural setting, in a world of combat, the male goat would break through this rancid hypnotic lust, "with a crash of horns against the horns/ Of the opposite enemy goat, / Thus hammering the mettle of goats into proof, and smiting out / The godhead of goats from the shock." A poem that is a hymn to higher consciousness!—in spite of its unusual subject matter, its relentless examination of the fenced-in life, the life of boundaries, domesticated procedures, in which the herd (which happens here to be female) dominates the individual, hypnotizing him with his own lust, imprisoning him inside the routine, ceaseless ritual of "procreation." There is probably more shrewd psychological analysis in this little-known poem than in any number of books, and it would be fascinating to examine Lawrence's assumptions here —and in the companion-piece, "The She-Goat"— along with the famous hypothesis Freud advanced in *Civilization and its Discontents*. For here, and probably only here, in a domesticated animal herd, do we find the absolutely uninhibited Id, never challenged even by another Id of comparable strength, but enjoying dominion over any number of sexual subjects; it is as if the rest of the world had been obliterated, all other rivals, all paternal figures, and the Super-Ego banished, forgotten. Civilization, Freud believed, rises out of the inexorable conflict between the desires of the individual and the restraining pressure of other individuals, a pressure that gradually evolves into "civilization" and becomes highly formalized, abstract, an enemy without an identity. Whatever the beauty and surprising variety of culture, it is the product solely of the sublimation (or frustration) of basic instincts.

Lawrence, however, understands that the release from all restraints, all conflict with the "Other," throws the individual back upon himself, his own instincts, and these become cruder and cruder, more and more routine, rancid, mesmerizing, in a way quite deathly—ironically enough, since the male goat is evidently fertilising the entire herd. But he is being used, he is reduced ultimately to "a needle of long red flint he stabs in the dark" while the she-goat "with her goaty mouth stands smiling the while as he strikes, since sure / He will never *quite* strike home. . . ." Exactly: the male will never "quite" mate with the female, under these circumstances, because he is undefined, only a dark instinct, "devilish," "malicious," stupid. During the later years of his life Freud was struggling with large, philosophical issues, trying to determine the relationship of the individual to "culture," and what the future must be if each person, retaining his basic opposition to all other persons, was finally unable to overcome his aggression. Hence, the "discontents." But the larger discontent of civilization was, in Freud's opinion, its apparently inevitable desire for destruction, even for self-destruction (aggression smothered and turned inward); given such a basic proposition, the future must be exactly like the past—endless wars, endless bloodshed, so long as human nature is "human nature." But Lawrence seems to have intuitively known that it is not the presence of a restraining or alien "enemy" that destroys man; it is the removal of this enemy. When the "Other" is obliterated the individual is also obliterated. It is ironic that Lawrence was known for most of his life as an "immoral" person, a writer of "pornography," when he seems to have understood the absolute need for sublimation of basic instincts. His admiration is for the ugly she-goat in the other poem, a marvelously individualized creature, really a personality in her own right. He is infuriated by her, he detests her as she pretends not to recognize him, then jumps "staccato" to the ground:

She trots on blithe toes,
And if you look at her, she looks back with a
   cold sardonic stare.
Sardonic, sardonyx, rock of cold fire.
See me? She says, *That's me!*

That's her.

Then she leaps the rocks like a quick rock,
Her backbone sharp as a rock,
Sheer will.

One is impressed continually by Lawrence's uncan-
ny instinct for what will bring out the best in him—
or perhaps the worst—his gravitation toward conflict,
drama, the stimulus that will "nudge" him out of his
blankness. In his own life he had so many enemies—
both personal and generalized—that he was saved
from the dull contented domesticity of the he-goat;
he admires the she-goat whom he really detests, or
detests half-seriously, because this is a creature whose
will is in opposition to his, a defiant cranky thing,
rather like the Lawrence of the biographies. It may
even be that Lawrence's ill health inspired in him a
kind of stubbornness, a willful defiance of any rou-
tine accommodation of his problem. Not only would
his diminution into a typical invalid, his restraining
of the more iconoclastic of his prophecies, satisfy his

enemies, but it would be too easy. He worships the sun, but not in any conventional neoprimitive manner —he worships it because it *is* hostile, inhuman, and unaccommodating. He was one of those unusual persons who exhibit a deep, unshakable faith in the inexplicable processes of life—or fate, or time, or accident—against which the individual must assert himself, in a continual struggle. Yeats vacillates between a desire for inert perfection (the golden bird, Byzantium itself, the "tower" of all the poems, the heavenly stupor to which Plotinus swims) and an eager, excited conviction that such perfection would be really hellish (as in the play *Where There is Nothing,* heaven is defined as a place where music is the "continual clashing of swords," and in the second of the "Plotinus" poems, "News for the Delphic Oracle," the languid paradise of the dead is jarred by "intolerable music" issuing from Pan's cavern).

To Lawrence, man's ideal state in nature is alienation—not total alienation, but a condition of disharmony that allows for the assertion of the personal self. He is not a Romantic, therefore, because he has no interest in regressing to a theoretical oneness with nature; he does not want to revive the primitive, as he makes abundantly clear in such stories as "The Woman Who Rode Away"—she rides away, after all, to her death. When an intelligent, civilized per-

43

son tries to behave as if he "knew" nothing, he becomes grotesque, stunted, like the unfortunate Hermione of *Women in Love,* who is probably the most abused character in all of Lawrence, savagely criticized by her lover, Birkin, for wanting sensuality in "that loathsome little skull of yours, that ought to be cracked like a nut." A similar woman in the short story "None of That" is punished even more savagely for her pretensions. It is wrong, I think, for critics to assume that Lawrence is venting his sadistic hatred of such women here; part of his energies are sadistic, of course, but essentially Lawrence is exorcising unclean, muddled, pseudo-primitive yearnings in himself, for he does reserve his most passionate scorn for people who mouth sentiments close to his own. Critics like Blackmur and Graham Hough, approaching Lawrence as an academic subject, fail to see how the creative artist shares to varying degrees the personalities of all his characters, even those whom he appears to detest—perhaps, at times, it is these characters he is really closest to. The declaration of one of his early essays, "The Crown," holds true for all of Lawrence's work: ". . . we are two opposites [lion and unicorn] which exist by virtue of our inter-opposition. Remove the opposition and there is a collapse, a sudden crumbling into universal darkness."[4]

This helps to explain the rather abrasive "She Said as Well to Me," which begins as a love poem—and quite nicely, the reader thinks—and then changes sharply into something else, when the lover turns upon his admiring beloved and forbids her to caress him and appreciate him: "it is an infamy." Just as she would hesitate to touch a weasel or an adder or a bull, she should hesitate to touch her lover, she should not assume that she knows him so intimately. (The title gains a deeper meaning, after the angry lesson of the poem is realized.) Man should not be easy in his loving, he should not be easy with himself, with nature; his inner sun is as hostile as the external sun, as dangerous and majestic.

Lawrence believed in the total spontaneous synthesis of "spiritual" and "sensual" love, indeed, but this love is not based on personalities, on anything personal, on what anyone happens to look like, or to believe, or to *be*. He is totally opposed to the waste of one's sacred energies with a crowd of people—he is a monogamist by nature (though he eloped with another man's wife)—and extremely critical of anyone who failed to live up to his ideal of permanent marriage. His "ideal" is at first highly comprehensible, at least to a century somewhat liberated from notions of shame or uneasiness about the physical side of life:

> At last I can throw away world without end, and
> meet you
> Unsheathed and naked and narrow and white;

45

At last you can throw immortality off, and I see
  you
Glistening with all the moment and all your
  beauty.

("Frohnleichnam")

But the personal, private self, the self with a name, is
to Lawrence a confining, a limitation, ultimately
deathly. This is what makes him so radical, and so
abrasive: his permanent love is based not upon the
daily, glistening body, it begins with this body, but
goes through it and transcends it, so that as the
permanently opposed entities of male and female
join, they create an inhuman, more-than-human
equilibrium, whether they want to or not. . . . There-
fore one marries only the person with whom he has
experienced this "inhuman" love, which is not
romantic love or perhaps even love at all. One mar-
ries, once. Lawrence's complete theology of love can
be found in Birkin's many passionate speeches in
Women in Love, which must be read, probably, be-
fore certain poems can be understood. The book of
poems called *Look! We Have Come Through!* is a
brutally honest recording of Lawrence's private ex-
perience, after he and Frieda have gone to Europe,
leaving her husband and children behind; it is not a
justification of this action—Lawrence never once in-
dicates any interest in the husband or children, cer-

46

tainly no guilt—but it is a remarkable book, perhaps the first of the frank, embarrassingly intimate confessional books of poetry commonplace today. But Lawrence achieves his higher, transcendental experience through the intimate, he evolves out of the love/ hate between himself and Frieda into an essentially inhuman sphere:

> We move without knowing, we sleep, and we
>   travel on. . . .
> And this is beauty to me, to be lifted and gone
> In a motion human inhuman, two and one
> Encompassed, and many reduced to none. . . .
>   ("One Woman to All Women")

The Unconscious is valued as the unknown oceanic source of all energies, good and bad, and Freud's heroic—or Faustian—desire to supplant the Id with the Ego would, of course, be an "infamy" to Lawrence, who had not Freud's day-to-day contact with people, and who could only project his own incredibly strong sense of self into everyone else. But, surely, it is a kind of infamous goal—"Where Id is, there shall Ego be"—if the "Id" is recognized as not essentially malevolent, and not essentially opposed to civilization. Freud in his deep, stark, stoical pessimism is, ironically, a kind of Romantic; Lawrence, individualized and conflict-ridden as he is, seems ultimately to be unclassifiable, really an optimist, if that word were not so inadequate. Even the "tragic joy" of Yeats (and, of course, Nietzsche—whom Yeats read carefully) is not quite Lawrence's joy. Lawrence is something *other.*

What is known and knowable, then, is automatically detested. This accounts for Ursula's rejection and rather cruel denunciation of her lover, so typically Victorian and career-oriented—poor Skrebensky, who would have been quite a daring figure in any other English novel, to have wandered into a novel by D. H. Lawrence! Ursula, like Lawrence himself, undergoes near-death and near-annihilation as a preparation for her tempestuous love for Birkin of *Women in Love,* Lawrence's explicit, heartlessly candid portrayal of himself in a dense, peopled world that does not always appreciate him. When Lawrence believes that he really *knows* something, himself, the results are usually catastrophic. When the rich, vulnerable humanity of Birkin, or Lawrence's bemused persona of *Birds, Beasts, and Flowers,* gives way to the absolute dictator Ramon, of *The Plumed Serpent,* it seems even to the most sympathetic reader that everything is lost, that Lawrence the artist has been murdered by Lawrence the dogmatist, whose cruelty or self-righteousness might be traced back, far back, into Lawrence's early career as a teacher— a half-serious observation, but one that makes sense if Ursula's experience as a teacher in *The Rainbow* is studied. When Lawrence worships the Other, his writing is at its finest; when he attempts to usurp the position of the Other, forcing his dreams of a metaphysical Utopia upon a God-enchanted, exotic land (it would have to be Mexico—not even the vast rawness of the American Southwest could have accommodated Lawrence's mad fantasy), it is mechanical and forced, embarrassingly bad. In the Quetzalcoatl state, which is dedicated to a resurrection of the body on earth, to a reawakening of man's fierce rapport with the universe, the voice of the sane Lawrence— "I think every man is a sacred and holy individual, *never* to be violated"—would be outshouted by the dictatorial Ramon, who desires nothing less than to be "lord of the day and night," controlling even his subjects' dreams. So Ramon and Lawrence must become neo-primitive, resurrecting an ancient Aztec myth and inventing new rituals—the kind of behavior Lawrence usually scorned, for its willful and Faustian desire to *control.* (After the egotistic fantasy of *The Plumed Serpent,* however, Lawrence turns to the very human, and in a way very subdued world of *Lady Chatterly's Lover,* where a few of the totalitarian ideas of Ramon turn up in the natural aristocrat, Mellors, but are sanely diminished; for Mellors, like Lawrence, recognizes the presence of enemies that will not be conquered, only challenged, by the "bright, quick flame" of human tenderness.)

49

Even at its worst, however, Lawrence's imagination is fertile. His invective against machinery never quite becomes entirely mechanical, itself, for in a perverse way he sometimes seems to share in the crazy energies of the machines, especially as they rush into self-destruction ("traffic will tangle up in a long-drawn-out crash of collision"—"The Triumph of the Machine"), and his retorts to Whitman and Jesus, among others, show how seriously he takes these apparently opposing points of view. It is clear that the simple act of writing was for Lawrence a triumph, a continuous triumph, an assertion of himself in which he can synthesize an extraordinary variety of selves— the "personal," the "transcendent-personal," the "sexual," the "social," the "artistic"—sometimes so excitedly calling attention to his foreground materials that we tend to forget that this *is* a form of art, perhaps the most sophisticated form of all. In both his fiction and his poetry Lawrence shows an awareness of the dichotomy of the illusions available to the imagination—the formal, structured work that exhibits content, and the exuberant, almost autonomous content that moves too fast to be structured.

Most of the poems, of course, are just as Lawrence judged them in "Chaos in Poetry": suffused fragments, visions "passing into touch and sound, then again touch and the bursting of a bubble of an image." But the finest poems achieve triumphs of both

50

content and form, and bear comparison with the greatest poems in our language. "The Ship of Death" is a "deepening black darkening" work of art that combines an intense, painful subjectivity and a mastery of objective form, the absolute conclusion of Lawrence's autobiographical work—one has only to imagine the *Complete Poems* without it, to realize how terrible a loss this would be. (More so than the loss of "Under Ben Bulben," perhaps.) Here, at the end of his life, the very consciously dying poet composes a poem to get him through his death, just as, years before, he composed "New Heaven and Earth" in an attempt to express his mystical experience. Like the beautiful "Bavarian Gentians," "The Ship of Death" is a construction by way of the artistic imagination of the attitude one must take toward death— that is, toward *dying,* the active, existential process of dying. And here Lawrence is equal to the challenge, as he has been equal to the challenge of expressing the mysteries of life throughout his career. "The Ship of Death" is about a symbolic ship, but a small one; the images of death are terrible, final, but they are familiar and small as well:

> Now it is autumn and the falling fruit
> and the long journey towards oblivion.
>
> The apples falling like great drops of dew
> to bruise themselves an exit from themselves.

51

> And it is time to go, to bid farewell
> to one's own self, and find an exit
> from the fallen self.

The "fallen self" builds its ship, its poem, to take it upon this journey into the unknown, into oblivion; it rejects once again the self-willed act of suicide: "for how could murder, even self-murder/ever a quietus make?" The symbol of the small ship is exactly right, it is exactly true to Lawrence's personality, for it is stocked with small, unpretentious items, a very human, humble vehicle:

> Now launch the small ship, now as the body dies
> and life departs, launch out, the fragile soul
> in the fragile ship of courage, the ark of faith
> with its store of food and little cooking pans
> and change of clothes,
> upon the flood's black waste . . . .

(Just so, Yeats declares as an *accomplished fact* his own death, and commands that his tombstone be made not of marble, but of limestone quarried nearby.) But Lawrence's death-journey ends at dawn, a "cruel dawn," out of which a mystical flush of rose glows, and there is some kind of renewal, "the whole thing starts again," as the frail soul abandons itself utterly to the Infinite: Lawrence's way of affirming, again, and at a time in his life when he might be tempted to deny it, the absolute mystery of the Other, which cannot be guessed and cannot be absorbed into the human soul. It is a kind of sensuous stoicism, an intelligent paganism—if the "pagan" were to be joined with the artistic soul, in having the consciousness required for the exertion of this will, this building of the individual's way into oblivion.

"The Ship of Death" goes beyond criticism, as it goes beyond the kind of poetry Lawrence usually wrote. A more characteristic poem—though not a lesser poem—is "Fish," which exhibits an almost mephistophelian sleight-of-hand, paying homage to the ineffable at the same time that the poet captures it. Here, content and form are perfectly joined. It is a remarkable kind of art, risky, chancy, characteristic of the best in *Birds, Beasts, and Flowers,* an attempt at the kind of mimetic exercise Birkin does in copying the Chinese drawing of geese in an early chapter of *Women in Love.* Lawrence stares down at the fish:

> Aqueous, subaqueous,
> Submerged
> And wave-thrilled.
> As the waters roll
> Roll you.
> The waters wash,
> You wash in oneness

And never emerge.

Lawrence is not assessing his own relationship to the fish, or converting them into symbols of human emotions. He is trying, trying very hard, to get into the suchness of fish:

> No fingers, no hands and feet, no lips;
> No tender muzzles,
> No wistful bellies,
> No loins of desire,
> None.

Only the fish in their "naked element": "Sway-wave. / Curvetting bits of tin in the evening light." The poem becomes an incantation, an extraordinary feat of magic[5] as the poet and his reader are transformed partly into fish: "Water-eager eyes, / Mouth-gate open / And strong spine urging, driving; / And desirous belly gulping." The poem goes on in this manner—it is one of his longer poems—with the roll of the waves themselves, the merging of self into anonymity, into shoals of fish. These fish, "born before God was love,"

> . . . drive in shoals.
> But soundless, and out of contact.
> They exchange no word, no spasm, not even

54

anger.
Not one touch.
Many suspended together, forever apart,
Each one alone with the waters, upon one wave
    with the rest.

A magnetism in the water between them only.

Lawrence sits in his boat on the Zeller lake and stares,
enraptured, down at the fish, saying finally to himself
Who are these? . . . for his heart cannot own them.
The reader has become half-transformed by the poem,
in a conventional response to the language, and now
he is shocked at the poet's sudden reversal, his dra-
matic statement:

I had made a mistake, I didn't know him,
  . . .
I didn't know his God,
I didn't know his God.

And now the poet is forced to recognize the terror of
the "pale of his being," which is only human, which
stares down into the world of fish and must realize
the limitations of the human soul, the fact that there
are "other Gods/ Beyond my range . . . ." He catches
a fish, unhooks it, feels the writhing life-leap in his
hand, and:

. . . my heart accused itself
Thinking: *I am not the measure of creation.*
This is beyond me, this fish.
His God stands outside my God.

Calm and matter-of-act as this statement is, it is
really revolutionary; it is a total rejection of that
dogma of the West that declares *Man is the measure
of all things.* How contemptible Lawrence found such
pronouncements, and how shrewdly he recognized
the melancholy nihilism behind them!—for it was
his life's pilgrimage to break through the confines of
the static, self-consuming self, in order to experience
the unfathomable power that transcended his own
knowledge of himself. Not "knowing" himself fully,
he cannot "know" and therefore violate anyone or
anything in nature.

One of our great prophetic books is *Women in
Love,* which attempts to dramatize Lawrence's faith.
However ironically its vision is contested by its plot,
it is a work meant to impress upon us the need for
men to join other men in a mysterious union, an im-
personal love, as they are conventionally joined with
women in order to transcend their limited selves.
Without this union and its transformation of the in-
dividual, the human race is doomed: but, since Law-
rence does not believe in tragedy, there is nothing
tragic about this predicament. Like most visionary

artists, he celebrates the life-force wherever it appears, even if it withdraws itself from the species to which he belongs. Here, in a passage at the conclusion of *Women in Love,* is the clearest statement of Lawrence's love for what may seem hostile, other, unhuman, but sacred—and it is a statement central to the visionary experience itself:

> If humanity ran into a *cul de sac,* and expended itself, the timeless creative mystery would bring forth some other being, finer, more wonderful, some new, more lovely race, to carry on the embodiment of creation. . . . The mystery of creation was fathomless, infallible, inexhaustible, forever. Races came and went, species passed away, but ever new species arose, more lovely, or equally lovely, always surpassing wonder. The fountain-head was incorruptible and unsearchable. It had no limits. It could bring forth miracles, create utter new races and new species, in its own hour, new forms of consciousness, new forms of body, new units of being. . . . To have one's pulse beating direct from the mystery, this was perfection, unutterable satisfaction. Human or inhuman mattered nothing. The perfect pulse throbbed with indescribable being, miraculous unborn species.

[1] See this very eloquent, passionate statement in *A Propos of Lady Chatterly's Lover:* "Sex is the balance of male and female in the universe. . . . Oh, what a catastrophe, what a maiming of love when it was made a personal, merely personal feeling, taken away from the rising and the setting of the sun, and cut off from the magic connexion of the equinox!" (p. 110, Penguin edition)

[2] Calvin Bedient, *Architects of the Self* (University of California Press, 1972), p. 179. The book is about the "ideal self" as imagined by George Eliot and E. M. Forster, in addition to Lawrence. Forster emerges as the most reasonable of the three—but perhaps the least exciting.

[3] Some critics, among them Graham Hough in *The Dark Sun* (London, 1968), see in Lawrence a "doctrinaire cruelty" in such stories as "The Princess," "None of That," etc., not taking into account how Lawrence imaginatively divided himself into the characters in his stories, both male and female. Lawrence's critical stance, which is often savage, must be understood in terms of the entire organic structure of the story, not simply its apparent "theme." If one sees that Lawrence *is* the white women he appears to be revenging himself upon, that he *is* "the Princess," whose father's ethic of the cold, locked-in ego dooms her to frigidity, the story comes alive as drama, and does not seem so polarized in its elements of "consciousness" and "instinct." Most novelists divide themselves up lavishly in their novels—it is an error to believe that Lawrence *is* Mellors any more than he is that strange, complex, and rather mad Sir Clifford Chatterly (who in one of his roles is a successful writer).

4 *Reflections of the Death of a Porcupine* (London, 1934), p. 6.

5 This dissolving of subject-into-object is a feat that few poets—especially those passionately involved with their own emotions—can achieve. The extraordinary empathy that James Dickey feels for nature has allowed him to create poems like "The Movement of Fish," "The Dusk of Horses," "Winter Trout," and many others, in which he gives us the sense of a magical transformation of the human ego. Western poetry, however, is generally dense with thought-out emotions, and even Imagism develops into a self-conscious aesthetic technique. It would be interesting to discuss poems like "Fish" in relation to Zen enlightenment poems, especially those that concentrate on realizing the absolute uniqueness of a single moment in nature, when poet and subject fuse together.

Printed August 1973 in Santa Barbara
for the Black Sparrow Press by Noel Young.
Design by Barbara Martin. This first edition
is published in paper wrappers; there are
300 hardcover copies numbered & signed by
the author; & 26 presentation copies
handbound in boards by Earle Gray lettered
& signed by the author.

239

JOYCE CAROL OATES was born in 1938 and grew up in the country outside Lockport, New York. She was graduated from Syracuse University in 1960 and received her Master's degree in English from the University of Wisconsin.

From the start of her writing career Ms. Oates has earned high literary acclaim. She was awarded a Guggenheim Fellowship in 1967-68 and the Richard and Hinda Rosenthal Foundation Award of the National Institute of Arts and Letters for her novel *A Garden of Earthly Delights* (1967). Her novel, *them,* won the National Book Award for fiction in 1970. *The Wheel of Love* (1970) contains many prize-winning stories. Her forthcoming novel, to be published in the fall of 1973, is called *Do With Me What You Will.*

Ms. Oates is an Associate Professor of English at the University of Windsor in Ontario.